Explore Your Senses

SMELL

by Laurence Pringle

BENCHMARK **B**OOKS

MARSHALL CAVENDISH
NEW YORK

The author wishes to thank Dr. Edward J. Kormondy, Chancellor and Professor of Biology (retired), University of Hawaii-Hilo/West Oahu for his careful reading of this text and his thoughtful and useful comments. The text has been improved by Dr. Kormondy's notes, however the author assumes full responsibility for the substance of the work, including any errors that may appear.

Benchmark Books
Marshall Cavendish Corporation
99 White Plains Road
Tarrytown, NY 10591

Library of Congress Cataloging-in-Publication Data
Pringle, Laurence P.
Smell / by Laurence Pringle.
p.   cm. — (Explore your senses)
Included bibliographical references and index.
Summary: Describes the sense of smell, how it works, and why it is important,
examining this sense in humans and a variety of other animals.
ISBN 0-7614-0737-5
1. Smell—Juvenile literature. [1. Smell. 2. Senses and sensation.] I. Title.
II. Series: Pringle, Laurence P.   Explore your senses.
QP458.P68   1999   612.8'6—dc21   98-29143   CIP   AC

Printed in Hong Kong

6   5   4   3   2   1

Photo research by Linda Sykes Picture Research, Hilton Head, SC

Cover photo: FPG International / Haroldo Castro
Picture credits: The photographs in this book are used by permission and through the
courtesy of: FPG International: 4 (bottom) Jim Cummins; Corbis: 7 (bottom)
NASA/Ressmeyer; Photo Edit: 4 (top) Robert Brenner; 5 (top), 17 David Young Wolff;
19 Novastock. Photo Researchers: 7 (top) Kent Wood; 13 George Haling; 20 Renee Lynn;
22 Michael Gadomski; 24 (bottom) John Kaprielian; 24 (top). Stock Boston: 5 (bottom)
Bob Daemmrich; 15 (top) Robert Crandall; 16 Carol and Mike Werner; 18 Seth Resnick;
25 Jeffrey Dunn; 27 Seth Resnick; 29 Bob Daemmrich. The Image Bank: 21 Janeart; 9 Paul
McCormick; 15 (bottom) Hank Delespinasse; 23 (top) Dag Sundberg; 23 (bottom) David
Hamilton; 26 Rita Maas.

Contents

Breathe in deeply through your nose. What do you smell? A person with a good sense of smell can detect ten thousand different odors!

Some of the odors, or scents, we smell are barely noticeable. You may have to bend close to a flower to sniff its faint scent. Other odors are strong. From far away you can detect the smell of wood smoke or a skunk.

Our sense of smell is important because it helps warn us of danger. We can tell when food is spoiled from the odor it gives off. The smell of smoke has awakened countless people—or sometimes, first, their dogs—and helped them escape from a house fire.

In everyday life we enjoy many smells—of freshly cut grass, brownies baking in the oven, even the smell of a new book in our hands. Our sense of smell has strong links with our memory. Sometimes the smell of a certain flower, or of the ocean, or of chalk dust will trigger a memory from long ago and far away.

You may have seen a dog following an invisible scent trail that you could not detect. A dog's sense of smell is at least ten times more powerful than ours. Many other animals also have a keener sense of smell than humans. Nevertheless, life is safer and more fun because of our ability to get information by sensing and remembering odors from the world around us.

Your Sense of Smell

Odors—strong or faint, foul or sweet—give people pleasure and sometimes warn them of danger.

The world is full of smells. Some odors delight us. Others may make us feel sick. And many, many others are totally unknown to people because humans have a rather weak sense of smell.

Some nonliving objects around us—rocks, glass, steel, plastic—give off no smell. Many chemicals are odorless to people, though we can smell chlorine that is added to the water of swimming pools. We can also smell ozone when it is especially abundant, during or just after a lightning storm.

Mostly we smell invisible *molecules* given off by living and once-living things. A molecule is the smallest possible amount of a substance that still has the characteristics of that substance. A molecule of water, for instance, is made up of two hydrogen atoms and one oxygen atom.

Molecules arise from your skin and hair, baking bread, rotting fruit, burning wood, and countless other materials, living and nonliving. We live in a constant bath of scent molecules.

The average person takes about 23,000 breaths each day. More than 400 cubic feet (10 cubic meters) of air is inhaled through the nose each day. The air we breathe is mostly molecules of nitrogen and oxygen gas, but it includes many odor molecules. Some may be very scarce—one molecule of a scent in a trillion other molecules—but your sense of smell can still detect them.

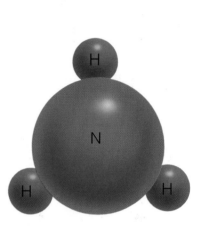

A molecule of ammonia, shown in this diagram, is very simple. (H stands for a hydrogen atom, N for nitrogen.) Many scent molecules are more complex, containing dozens of atoms.

The Source of Scents

Lightning breaks oxygen molecules apart, and some of the free molecules join to form ozone, which has a metallic odor. Travelers in space (below) may not detect odors well because the lack of gravity affects the movement of scent molecules in the air.

When you inhale, a sample of the outside air goes deep inside your nose for just a second or two on its way to your lungs. In an instant, scent molecules in the air are intercepted, messages about them are sent to your brain, and you recognize the odor.

Air that enters your two *nostrils* flows into a pair of *nasal cavities. Turbinate* bones project into each nasal cavity, forcing the air to go through a kind of maze. This helps warm the air. This also helps clean the air before it reaches your lungs. One defense against irritating odors and dust is the *trigeminal nerve cells* that line part of your nasal cavities. When these nerve cells, or neurons, are irritated, you sneeze. This blasts the annoying and possibly harmful substances out of your nose.

The main defense against dust and bacteria in the air is a slimy fluid called *mucus* that lines the inside surfaces of the nasal cavities. Tiny hairlike structures called *cilia* move back and forth, causing the mucus to flow toward your throat. Every day the inner walls of your nasal cavities produce a quart of mucus. Every day this mucus flows unnoticed down your throat to your stomach. It carries away dirt and germs from the air you breathe.

Most of your nasal cavity surface is devoted to cleaning the air. Only a small part, deep within your nose, senses odors. (From the outside, it is located just behind and above the bridge of your nose.)

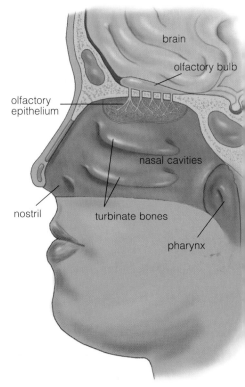

brain

olfactory bulb

olfactory epithelium

nasal cavities

nostril

turbinate bones

pharynx

Deep Within Your Nose

Also, only a small fraction of inhaled air reaches this deepest part of the nasal cavities. During normal breathing, as little as 2 percent of inhaled air reaches this deep area. When you give a strong sniff, about 20 percent of the air reaches your scent detectors.

When you breathe through your mouth, or take in air while talking or eating, some air rises up your *pharynx*—the passageway from the back of your mouth to the back of your nose. This air, too, contains scent molecules that can be captured and identified.

Odor-sensitive cells are concentrated in two tiny patches called the *olfactory epithelium* (which means "smelling skin"). Each is about the size of a small postage stamp. Each is covered with sticky mucus. Odor molecules in the air are caught in the mucus. This is an important step because the scent molecules must be wet in order to be detected by the neurons in the epithelium.

The color of the olfactory epithelium is a clue to how well a person or an animal detects smells. *Albino* people, who lack normal color everywhere on their bodies, have a very poor sense of smell. The epithelium of most humans is pale yellow. People with a deeper yellow epithelium have a stronger sense of smell. In the noses of cats, dogs, and other mammals that have a much keener sense of smell than humans, the olfactory epithelium is dark yellow or even brown.

The red fox can detect many more scents than people can.

Compared with seeing and hearing, the sense of smell is simple and direct. One end of the neurons that detect odors dangles down into the mucus of the olfactory epithelium. The other end of these neurons passes through tiny holes in a thin bone of your skull and reaches right into your brain. No other sense has such a direct link between the outside environment and the brain.

Your sense of smell is remarkable in another way. If neurons in your eyes and ears are damaged, they cannot be replaced. The odor-sensing neurons in your nose are replaced every month or two. This is necessary because they are not as well protected as other kinds of neurons and are sometimes damaged.

Five million of these neurons lie deep in each of your nasal cavities. Cilia reach out from each neuron. It is the cilia that first touch odor molecules. In the neuron, information about the odor is changed to an electrical signal that is passed to the brain's *olfactory bulbs*. These are two bundles of nerve fibers, one for each nasal cavity. Each bulb is about the size of a small grape. The olfactory bulbs lie at the base of the front of the brain.

If the process of smelling were interrupted at this point, you would know you had smelled something but would not know *what*. To answer this question, an electrical message travels from the olfactory bulbs to the area of your brain that is involved with memo-

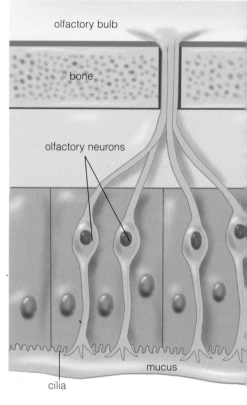

olfactory bulb

bone

olfactory neurons

mucus

cilia

Your Brain Smells!

ries and emotions. There the odor is identified.

So smelling actually occurs in your brain, not your nose. Just as seeing, hearing, tasting, and touching occur in the brain, so, too, does smelling.

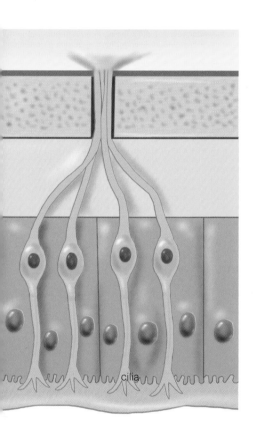

Scent messages are sent deep inside the brain to the center of memories and emotions.

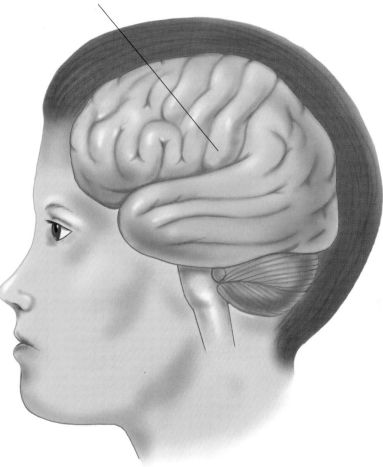

Our sense of smell has not been studied nearly as much as our senses of sight and hearing. Many puzzles remain. In recent years, however, scientists have made progress in better understanding how it works.

Scientists have discovered that only about a thousand kinds of neurons make up the total of 5 million neurons in the human nose. Each of the thousand neurons responds to just one type of odor molecule.

This is puzzling, since humans can identify far more than a thousand smells. How can we know as many as ten thousand odors with only a thousand kinds of odor-detecting neurons? The answer, scientists believe, is this:

An odor is usually made up of several molecules. Some scents may be made up of more than a dozen molecules. When you inhale and these molecules touch the cilia of neurons, some of the neurons "recognize" the one scent molecule they know. This has been compared to a key fitting into a lock.

When neurons "recognize" a scent molecule, they respond by relaying a message to the olfactory bulb. There the messages from many neurons enter little round *glomeruli*. In all, there are about two thousand glomeruli in the human brain. (A single one is called a glomerulus.) The glomeruli act like a telephone switchboard or relay station. They receive

Scent molecules may match up with neurons—like keys fitting into locks.

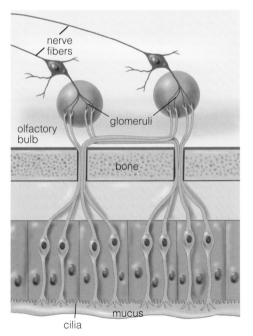

nerve fibers

olfactory bulb

glomeruli

bone

mucus

cilia

Making Sense of Scents

messages from different kinds of neurons, combine the information from them, then send a message through nerve fibers to other parts of the brain.

Understanding how scent-detecting neurons work also helps explain a condition known as *odor fatigue*. Everyone with a sense of smell has experienced odor fatigue. It can happen with a pleasant smell or a bad-smelling one. You may have entered a bakery and noticed delicious smells, or entered a home or other building and noticed a strong, unpleasant smell. As time passes, however, you could hardly smell it.

The strong odor was still there, and a newcomer would notice it upon arriving, but you no longer smell it because of odor fatigue. This occurs when scent molecules have connected—like a key in a lock—with all of the neurons that can receive them. They have all sent messages to the glomeruli. A natural chemical in the body called an *enzyme* then stops the neurons from sending more messages about the odor.

Odor fatigue can be a blessing for someone who works in a grossly smelly place. On the other hand, some people who work in candy factories say that sweet smells and even the scent of chocolate lose their appeal, until they go on a long vacation.

A bakery customer notices strong aromas, but bakery workers do not because of their odor fatigue.

The next time you are really enjoying the taste of a favorite food, try this: With a forefinger and thumb, pinch your nostrils closed. What happens to the flavor of the food?

Or try this: Cut slices of a firm apple and similar slices of a raw potato. Offer the different slices, one at a time, to friends or family members whose eyes are covered and whose nostrils are closed. Can they tell apple from potato?

Although humans can recognize thousands of odors, they recognize only a few tastes. Most of what we call the flavor of food is actually its aroma. Even as you bring food to your mouth, scent molecules from it enter your nostrils and rise up your nasal cavities.

As soon as the food is in your mouth, more scent molecules are released and rise up the pharynx. You exhale, and the molecules touch scent detectors as air flows out of your nose.

When you have a head cold, the mucus deep in your nose thickens. This makes it difficult for the cilia of neurons to detect odor molecules. You may notice that your sense of smell doesn't work very well. Also, foods seem to have lost their flavor. Of course the foods are as tasty as ever, but your clogged-up nose keeps you from enjoying their flavors.

Smell and Taste

When you eat, scents from the food affect its taste. To test this idea, eat some jelly beans with distinctive flavors. Then, without looking, pick up one jelly bean and eat it while pinching your nostrils closed. Can you still identify its flavor?

Smells are difficult to describe. We can put specific names to colors, tastes, and things we touch. Think of an orange—its color, flavor, and its smooth but slightly bumpy surface. However, there is no simple single word to describe the smell of an orange. Tests show that people can detect a great variety of smells, but have trouble putting a name to each one.

Odors are usually described by using the name of the thing being smelled, or by comparing it to another smell. We say that odors are like rotten eggs, tar, honey, or a wet dog. Or we describe them by saying how they make us feel, for example, a delightful smell or a disgusting one.

For more than two thousand years, people have tried to find a way to classify smells. In 1752 a Swedish botanist named Carolus Linnaeus divided all odors into seven different groups. They were: aromatic, fragrant, ambrosial (musky), alliaceous (garlicky), hycrine (cheesy), repulsive, and nauseous.

A plan that divided smells into nine groups was proposed by Dutch scientist Hendrik Zwaardemaker in 1895. They were:

1. aromatic (almond, cloves, lemon)
2. fragrant (flowers, vanilla)
3. ambrosial (musky)
4. ethereal (fruits, resins)

An orange smells like . . . an orange. How else would you describe its scent?

Naming What We Smell

5. alliaceous (garlic, onion, chlorine)
6. empyreumatic (roasted coffee, burned substances)
7. caprylic (cheese, sweat)
8. repulsive (narcotics, bedbugs)

Early in the twentieth century, in 1916, a German scientist named Hans Henning divided all smells into six groups: floral, fruity, resinous, spicy, putrid, and burned. He arranged them on a figure with six corners, with one of the smells at each corner. He believed that this diagram showed how smells are related. For example, he placed the odor of cloves between floral and spicy, but closer to spicy.

However, no system for classifying all smells has worked very well. Some odors just don't seem to fit into any category. And people disagree about smells. Long ago, Hendrik Zwaardemaker wrote that the bedbug, once a common household pest, gave off a repulsive odor. Bedbugs are scarce these days, but some people who have sniffed them say they smell like raspberries.

How would you describe the odor of a sweaty sock?

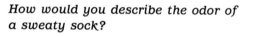

Of all senses, the sense of smell is most closely tied to our memories. You probably have had the experience of a scent stirring up old memories and feelings. They may be pleasant or unpleasant. Perhaps a certain food once made you sick. Just the smell of it is enough to give you a funny feeling in your stomach. On the other hand, the aroma of baking bread may bring back memories and feelings about good times you had in your grandmother's kitchen.

If you ask your memory for a picture of a friend's face or the sound of her or his voice, your brain can usually give you these sights and sounds. You cannot, however, imagine a scent the way you can imagine a face or voice. First you smell the scent, then the memory comes.

Studies have compared how well people remember smells and pictures. In one test, people were shown a series of photographs, then were asked questions about the pictures four months later. They recalled seeing about half of the photos. However, when asked if they recognized a variety of scents, they remembered about two out of every three a whole year after they had first smelled them. Unlike other senses, there is very little loss of odor memories.

The sense of smell's strong link with memory helps protect people from harm. As young children, people learn that certain smells can mean danger.

Odors stimulate memories of good food and good times, and also memories of spoiled, unsafe food.

Scent Memories

These include smoke from a fire and the smell of food spoiled by bacteria. For their own safety it is important for people to be able to recall certain odor memories, even though they may not have smelled them in many years.

Fortunately, an odor we haven't smelled for a long time can also produce a vivid, pleasing memory. Perhaps you have had that experience. What kind of smell was it? Whether a food smell, a plant smell, or the scent of a whole place, an odor can take us back for a visit in our memories.

People Vary

The skunk is often used as a symbol of a truly bad smell. However, some people enjoy the scent of a skunk. People differ in odors they like or dislike, and also in their smelling ability.

From birth, some people cannot smell certain odors. They seem to lack some specific odor-sensitive neurons. Also, little children do not seem to pay much attention to smells. They sometimes play with their own feces. Older children and adults find the odor of most animal feces disgusting. However, this isn't true everywhere in the world. The Masai people of East Africa sometimes dress their hair with cow droppings. They like both the color and the smell that results.

Research shows that females have a better sense of smell than males. This is true of both five-year-olds and adults. Whether men or women, people reach the peak of their smell-sensing powers between the ages of twenty and forty. Then the ability to detect scents gets weaker and weaker with age.

Although the human sense of smell is weak compared with many animals, people do show some remarkable sensing skills with their noses. At birth, human infants cannot see well but their sense of smell is already developed. They use it to find their mother's breast to nurse. Studies have shown that a mother's sense of smell can be sensitive to certain odors. Mothers who were given the clothes of

The skunk's strong odor, sprayed in self-defense, is enjoyed by some people.

in What and How They Smell

several babies to sniff could recognize those worn by their own babies. They could usually identify a T-shirt of an older child by its odor. In one study, sixteen out of eighteen mothers could identify which of their two children had worn a T-shirt.

People are also able to recognize other loved ones by their special smell. Everyone has a scent "signature." Some of it comes from foods, favorite soaps, and other scent sources in the home. Most of it comes from the skin, where glands give off faint aromas that give people their distinctive scents. Bacteria, however, can change this odor, producing a strong smell that many people find unpleasant. However, it is other faint smells that give people their distinctive scents.

Both mothers and infants use their sense of smell to recognize one another.

With a limited sense of smell, people can only imagine what dogs and other animals learn from the odors around them. A dog that could smell only as well as a human would be terribly handicapped. It would be unable to detect and understand a wealth of information from other dogs and from its surroundings.

Bloodhounds are famous for their ability to follow a faint trail of odors, but a healthy dog of any breed can easily "out-smell" a human. Most dog breeds have long snouts that are packed with as many as 200 million odor detectors. (Remember, people have about 10 million.) Dogs and their wild relatives (including wolves, jackals, and foxes) rely more on their sense of smell than on sight. The largest part of their brains is devoted to interpreting odors.

Cats have about the same number of odor-sensing cells as dogs. Both also have a secret weapon, called the *vomeronasal organ*. Although many mammals and reptiles also have this organ, your best chance to see it in use is to watch a cat.

When a cat finds an especially interesting odor to investigate, it opens its mouth and curls its lips into an expression like a smile. When you see a cat with this strange look on its face, you know that it is getting even more scent information than usual. It inhales air into its mouth so that scent molecules reach neurons that line two small openings in the

Scents inhaled into a cat's mouth reach a special smelling organ in the roof of its mouth.

Amazing Animal Noses

roof of its mouth—its vomeronasal organ.

Snakes also have vomeronasal organs. Many kinds of snakes catch their prey by following scent trails. A snake smells through its nostrils but also detects scents by flicking its two-pronged tongue in and out of its mouth. Scent molecules in the air cling to the wet tongue. The tongue flicks back into the mouth, and the snake rubs the molecules in the two little pockets of the Vomeronasal organ in the roof of its mouth.

Name almost any animal, and it has a better sense of smell than you. A pig can detect the odor of an edible mushroom, the truffle, beneath the soil. A male moth can sense a special aroma given off by a female moth 3 miles (5 kilometers) away.

Animals that can see very well usually do not have a good sense of smell. Their vision enables them to find food and mates, and to avoid danger. Monkeys, like humans, have good vision and do not have a powerful sense of smell. Neither do birds. Most birds have excellent vision. Those that do not rely more on their sense of smell.

Vultures have large nostrils and many more scent-detecting neurons than most birds. While a vulture soars high in the sky, its sense of smell is keen enough to detect the scent of a dead animal. Then it circles lower and lower, zeroing in on the source of the aroma.

Snakes take scent molecules from the air with their tongues.

Pigs are able to detect faint scents in the soil where they root for food.

If you accidentally disturb a hidden nest of yellow jackets (a kind of hornet), you may get stung unless you run away fast. In defending their home and young, the yellow jackets give off scent molecules called *pheromones*. The scent is an alarm signal. It is a call to action. Yellow jackets rush to defend their colony, ready to sting.

A pheromone is an airborne chemical signal from one animal to others of its kind. Pheromones are vital in the lives of many kinds of animals. Some mammals, including dogs and wolves, mark the borders of their territory with pheromones in their urine. Both urine and droppings contain pheromone information about an animal's identity, including whether it is a male or female. Like love letters, pheromones carry key messages between male and female animals during mating season. If hamsters are kept from smelling the odor of their mates, they lose all interest in them.

Pheromones are so important in the lives of many insects that half of all the neurons in their tiny brains are scent detectors. This is especially true of ants, termites, bees, and other insects that live in colonies. Pheromones carry all sorts of messages among these social insects. An ant that dies gives off a special odor that tells worker ants to remove it from the colony. When a live ant is marked with some of the "dead ant" pheromone, the workers

Yellow jackets give off scent signals to others in their colony.

Cats send and receive scent messages every day.

24

toss it out. The live ant returns. It is carried out again. This continues until the smell-of-death pheromone wears off.

Many mammals have scent glands that emit pheromones. On lemurs the scent glands are on the tail and front legs. On elephants they are on the head, between the eyes and ears. On cats they are on the cheeks, chin, and eyebrow area, and at the base of the tail. House cats rub their faces and rumps against objects, including the legs of people. They leave pheromone messages that say, "I was here," "I belong here," and "This is mine."

Humans, too, produce scents that are pheromones. The odors do not seem to affect people nearly as much as pheromones affect other animals. This is still being studied. Some scientists think that human pheromones are detected by vomeronasal organs. In people these tiny pits are located just inside each nostril. However, more research is needed to tell whether these organs work as they do in other animals.

Some experts think that kissing may be a way for people to inhale scent messages from others. In several languages around the world, the word for "kiss" means "smell." And in some cultures, people greet each other by rubbing noses or sniffing faces.

Is kissing also a way to send and receive scent messages?

A thousand varieties of perfume are for sale around the world. In the United States alone, people spend 5 billion dollars a year on perfume. And the perfume business is small compared with many other uses of scents that are aimed at making people and products smell good.

People buy shampoo that cleans their hair and leaves a pleasant aroma. They buy deodorants, hand creams, after-shave lotions, and other products that give them an appealing smell—according to the advertisements for the products. But these are just a few of the ways in which manufacturers use scents.

Think of all the items in your house that have fragrances added. A short list would include dish-washing soap (often lemon scented), plastic trash bags, toilet paper, wrapping paper, dolls, magazines, and cat litter. Cats like the smell of anise seeds, which have a licorice scent, so cat litter usually smells faintly of anise.

Other scents are usually added to cat litter to mask the smells of cat feces and urine. This is called odor masking. Thousands of years ago, the original use of perfumes was for covering up smells. Today, odor masking is sometimes used in workplaces to help employees who must work among bad smells. People who sell used cars sometimes try to mask odors, too. They spray the inside of used cars with an odor that is like the smell of a brand-new car.

Perfume-making is just one business that uses odors in its products.

Scents and Dollars

In some shopping malls, a faint cinnamon scent swirls through the air because studies have shown this encourages people to shop. Cinnamon itself may not be used because scent makers have found ways to make artificial odors. This is important because some scents that are used widely in perfumes come from rare plants and animals.

One such smell is civet. Another is musk. One originally came from glands of the African civet cat, the other from glands of the male Asian musk deer. Long ago these animals were the only source of odors that were used in many perfumes. They were killed for their scent glands. Fortunately for these animals, their odors are now manufactured, thanks to chemists who work in the big business of scent making.

People are hired to judge the scent appeal of many products—in this photo, of dog food.

H ave you ever scratched a magazine advertisement or a sticker, sniffed the place where you scratched, and smelled perfume, or lemon, or another odor? "Scratch-and-sniff" is another way to advertise products or to make them more appealing. Artificial scents are sealed inside microscopic capsules. The scents are released when you break the capsules open with a fingernail.

"Scratch-and-sniff" has another use: to test the smelling ability of people. A test with fifty odors is used to help doctors discover if their patients have a normal sense of smell.

About 2 million people in the United States suffer from *anosmia*. The word means "without smell," and these people cannot smell anything. At least another million people have an impaired sense of smell. Added together, this is a small part of the population. Still, these people suffer because food is almost tasteless to them. Also, they are at risk because they cannot smell smoke from a fire, a gas leak, or the odor of spoiled food.

Some people are born with no sense of smell. Others suffer from anosmia because of their age. Most people over the age of eighty have a weak sense of smell.

Young people sometimes lose some or all of their sense of smell from an accident or illness. A head injury can damage the nerves that carry scent

As they age, even people in good health gradually lose some of their sense of smell.

Care of Your Sense of Smell

messages to the brain. Infections can harm scent-detecting neurons. So can inhaling air pollutants, harsh-smelling chemicals, and tobacco smoke. Smokers lose some of their ability to detect odors. As a result, unpleasant smells don't bother smokers as much as they do nonsmokers. However, smokers miss the full strength of life's good smells, too.

Although no one can stop aging, some of the threats to your sense of smell can be avoided. A head injury is the most common cause of anosmia among young people. Always wear a helmet while bike riding. Wear protective headgear while playing football and other contact sports too, even if you are just in your own backyard. And see a doctor if you have an especially bad head cold, to avoid harm to your scent-detecting neurons from infection.

A bad cold with a mucus-loaded nose keeps us from smelling—and tasting. It reminds us of what we are missing—of life's wonderful aromas, of scent memories, and of the sense of smell we take for granted.

Protective helmets can help avoid injuries that cause loss of the sense of smell.

albino—a human or animal that lacks normal color. Albino people have very pale skin and hair, and also a weak sense of smell.

anosmia—loss of one's sense of smell.

cilia—microscopic, hairlike growths on the outer surface of cells.

enzyme—a natural chemical in the body (a protein) that is vital in the inner workings of an animal's body.

glands—organs that release chemicals within the body that affect digestion and other processes, or that release chemicals outside the body (pheromones) that carry messages to other animals.

glomeruli—round bodies inside the olfactory bulbs of the brain that play a key role in making sense of information from nerve cells that receive odors.

mammals—animals with backbones that nurse their young with milk.

molecule—the smallest possible amount of a substance that still has the chemical characteristics of the substance.

mucus—a sticky fluid given off by glands that protects surfaces within the body. In the nose, mucus traps dust and bacteria. It also moistens scent molecules so they can be detected by odor-sensitive neurons, or nerve cells.

nasal cavities—twin chambers, one for each nostril, through which inhaled air flows on its way to the lungs.

nostrils—the openings to the nasal cavities, located at the front of the nose.

odor fatigue—a condition that occurs when a person notices an odor but then smells it less even though it is still present.

Glossary

olfaction—the sense of smell.

olfactory bulbs—bundles of nerve fibers at the bottom front of the brain, from which messages about scents received in the nose are sent to other parts of the brain.

olfactory epithelium—an area located deep in each nasal cavity that is packed with scent-detecting neurons. Odors detected in this area are identified as specific smells in the brain.

pharynx—the passageway between the nasal cavities and the back of the mouth cavity.

pheromones—airborne chemicals that carry messages from one animal to others of its kind. Dogs, other mammals, and many insects find mates by sensing pheromones.

trigeminal nerve cells—nerve cells, or neurons, that respond to strong, irritating scent molecules, and that may trigger a sneeze. They are part of the body's defense against dangerous substances.

turbinates—thin, flat bones inside the nose that guide the flow of air that is inhaled.

vomeronasal organs—a pair of openings lined with scent-detecting neurons in the roof of the mouth of cats, many other mammals, and reptiles and amphibians.

Index

Page numbers for illustrations are in boldface.

FEB   2001